ALFRED'S DRUM METHOD
COMPLETE

Sandy Feldstein

Dave Black

Special Corps-Style Section
by Jay Wanamaker

ISBN-10: 0-7390-8893-9
ISBN-13: 978-0-7390-8893-7

TABLE OF CONTENTS

INTRODUCTION

Sandy Feldstein and Dave Black gave the world of drumming a most precious gift in the form of *Alfred's Drum Method*. I can think of no better-paced or more logical sequence of pedagogical studies than those contained in this book. Indeed, this has proven to be more than just a book. *Alfred's Drum Method* codifies what a book that teaches music should be: clear explanations, coupled with perfectly appropriate exercises that build the best possible foundation for any aspiring drummer. *Alfred's Drum Method* is timeless. It paved the way for all drum method authors who followed, and it will continue to shine the brightest light on the path to drumming, most likely more than all other method books combined.

Sandy's legacy is so well presented and preserved in these pages, and Dave's continued stewardship of the method and its publication serves as an inspiration to all of us who care about the passing on of drumming information. Bravo, Sandy and Dave, and congratulations to *Alfred's Drum Method*!

—**Peter Erskine**
Los Angeles, 2012

ACKNOWLEDGEMENTS

The authors wish to thank the following people for their invaluable assistance:
Scott Lavine, Joel Leach, Christopher Leach (model), J. Jeff Leland (photographer), John O'Reilly and Joe Vasile.

We would also like to give a special thanks to everyone who provided a testimonial, quote or endorsement. We are truly grateful for your support.

FOREWORD

Alfred's Drum Method Complete has been designed to provide the student and teacher with a comprehensive method to assist the student in his/her pursuit of becoming a well-rounded percussionist. The first half of the book provides how-to knowledge regarding drum care, tuning, plus stick and drumhead selection. The second half of the book includes materials which explore traditional rudimental style, corps style and orchestral style, plus sections which deal with accessory instruments and multiple-percussion techniques. Each page is designed as a complete lesson; materials are combined at the end of each lesson in a logical and musical solo passage. There is also an entire drum solo at the end of each complete section which may be used for contest purposes.

The method also includes actual drum parts from well-known marches and concert band pieces. Although some have been edited so they can be played by the beginning student, they remain musically faithful to the original band pieces. Students may wish to play along with the numerous available recordings of some of the classic marches.

Students must set aside a reasonable amount of practice time on a regular basis in order to achieve best results. We recommend no less than 30 minutes per day, although some lessons will require more time. When practicing, students should play each exercise as written, being certain that proper hand, finger, arm and body positions are maintained at all times. The authors have made a concerted effort to present the material in an interesting and musical manner. We hope you'll find the book to be an enjoyable experience in your pursuit of musical excellence.

THE SNARE DRUM

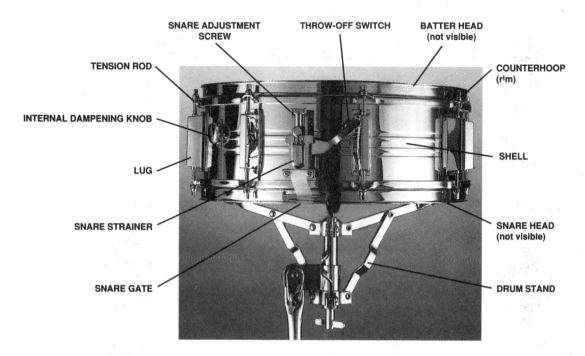

SNARE ADJUSTMENT SCREW — THROW-OFF SWITCH — BATTER HEAD (not visible) — TENSION ROD — COUNTERHOOP (rim) — INTERNAL DAMPENING KNOB — SHELL — LUG — SNARE STRAINER — SNARE HEAD (not visible) — SNARE GATE — DRUM STAND

Tuning the Snare Drum

The top head of a snare drum is referred to as the batter head. The bottom head is called the snare head. Heads are held in place by rims and can be adjusted by means of threaded rods attached to the lugs on the side of the snare drum. The number of rods and lugs attached to the snare drum depends upon the size of the drum but there are usually 8 to 10 on most drums. Adjusting these rods alters the tension of the drum heads.

When tuning the snare drum we suggest that you start with the batter side first. Tune the head by using the cross system method of tensioning. This method maintains even tensioning around the drum throughout the entire tuning process. Tap the head with a drum stick about two inches from each rod to be certain that the pitch is consistent all the way around the drum. If it is not, adjust individual tension rods as needed.

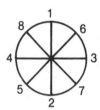

Cross tension system of tensioning

You may also tune the drum sequentially, tightening the rods as you move in a circular fashion around the drum. Tighten each screw one-half turn (or twist of the wrist) each time. Do this repeatedly until the drum head feels firm. Be sure you don't tension any lug more than the others. Tap the head with a drum stick about two inches from each rod to be certain that the pitch is consistent all the way around the drum.

Clockwise system of tensioning

Tuning the Snare Drum (continued)

The snare head is tensioned in much the same manner as was the batter head. You may have to use one hand to lift the snares from the surface of the head while tensioning with the other hand to avoid snare rattle as you proceed. Tension the snare head firmly, but be sure that it is able to vibrate freely against the snares.

After achieving the desired pitch and tension for both heads, tap the batter head with a drumstick while adjusting the "snare adjustment screw" until the snares have been brought into contact with the snare head and the desired sound has been achieved. Be careful not to over-tighten the drum heads and the snares or you might restrict the sound of the drum. Remember, sound is produced by allowing the heads and snares of the drum to vibrate freely. Test continually by tapping the head lightly with a drumstick.

Drum Heads

The majority of drummers today use plastic drum heads exclusively. There are a wide variety of such heads on the market today; the drummer will have to choose the drum head which will best fit his/her needs. Skin heads, once the only kind available, are no longer very popular due to both price and maintenance factors.

Plastic heads become soiled after continued usage; they may be cleaned with a damp cloth and mild soap.

The Snares

Wire snares are most commonly used on concert or kit drums. They are not affected by weather conditions and require very little up-keep.

Gut snares are most commonly used on parade/field drums where a crisp sound and higher volume levels are required. Since gut snares are easily affected by weather conditions (such as humidity), extra care is required in maintaining them. Regardless of the type, snares should not be too tight; they should be adjusted so that the drum "speaks freely" and does not choke.

Maintaining Your Snare Drum

Regular cleaning of your snare drum will help prolong both the life and the quality of the drum.

Wood parts may be cleaned with a damp cloth and mild soap if necessary; mild furniture polish may be applied to wood surfaces. Metal shells and hoops may be cleaned with a damp cloth or metal polish. Pearl finishes may be cleaned with a damp cloth. Tension rods should be lubricated with Vaseline or light grease and moving parts such as the snare strainer and control arm should be lubricated with light machine oil.

GETTING READY TO PLAY

Holding the Sticks

There are many ways of holding drumsticks, depending on the style of drumming on which you are concentrating. The authors recommend that the beginning student start with the traditional grip. Developing the proper position and manner of holding the drumsticks is very important in the development of proper technique, attack, and control. Check periodically to make sure that the sticks are being held correctly, that the arm position is as it should be and that the general position of the body is correct. Practicing in front of a mirror can be helpful in this regard.

The Right Hand

The stick should be thought of as a natural extension of the arm. 1) The stick is gripped between the thumb and first joint of the index finger, one third of the distance from the butt end of the stick. The other fingers will be used to help control the stick. 2) Close the other fingers loosely around the stick. 3) Turn the hand so that the back of the hand is facing upward when playing. The stick should be in an approximate line with the wrist and arm.

The Left Hand

1) Place the stick in the socket between the thumb and first finger, with one third of the stick (from the butt end) extending behind the hand. The grip should be just tight enough to cause a slight drag if one were to try to pull the stick from the hand. 2) The first two fingers should rest lightly on top of the stick (the first more than the second) to act as a guide. The stick should rest across the third finger which will act as a support. The fourth finger should rest against the third finger.

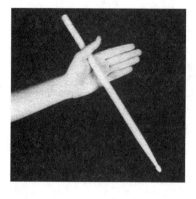
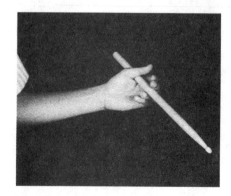
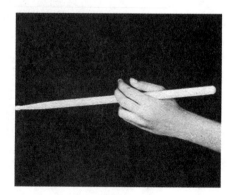

Matched Grip

In both hands, the sticks are gripped between the thumb and first joint of the index finger, one third of the distance from the butt end of the stick (see right hand grip description above for details).

Striking the Drum

When resting on the drum head, the sticks should approximate a 90 degree angle. They should strike near (but not on) the center of the drum head. The space in which they strike should be no larger than 1½ to 2 inches in diameter. Since the pitch of the drum varies considerably as you move from the center of the drum head to the rim, it is important that each stick be kept an equal distance from the center of the head so that an even tone is produced. (There may be times, however, when you will want to play a passage "near the edge.")

Sound is produced by striking the top head. This sets the air inside the drum in motion, which causes the bottom head and snares to vibrate. Because of this, the sticks must be allowed to rebound from the head as quickly as possible.

THE STROKE is produced by a turn of the wrist in a down-up motion.
1. Place the tip of the stick on the head.
2. Turn the wrist so the tip of the stick is as far away from the head as possible.
3. Play the stroke (down-up) striking the head and returning immediately to the up position.

1.  2., 3.

1.  2., 3.

When alternating strokes, the right (left) stick strikes the drum and rebounds to a position approximately two inches above the head. When the left (right) stick comes down, the right stick goes from the low position to the full up position.

THE BASS DRUM

The bass drum is the largest member of the drum family. Its main function is to hold a steady tempo and to help with phrasing and accents. The bass drum should be positioned so that the music stand and the director may be seen in a straight line.

The Size of the Bass Drum

The size of the bass drum should be determined by the type of playing and by the size of the musical organization in which it is to be used. The depth of the drum should not be over one-half of the diameter of the head.

Tuning the Bass Drum

It's important that the tension be equalized around the entire circumference to obtain the best tone. This is accomplished in much the same manner as with snare drum tuning.

The tone of the bass drum should be "dark" and low in pitch. If the head is too loose, it will vibrate lifelessly; if too tight, it will ring too much. Both heads should be at approximately the same pitch for maximum resonance.

Where to Strike the Drum

When struck in the exact center, the drum head produces a "dull thud;" the area near the rim produces a high pitched ringing tone. The best playing spot is about halfway between the center and the edge of the drum. This may vary depending on the musical setting and the size of the ensemble.

The Bass Drum Beater

There are many types of bass drum beaters available; since the beater affects the drum's tone significantly, it is very important that careful thought be given to the selection process.

Although the common double-headed lamb's wool beater is acceptable, many people feel it does not produce the best tone. A somewhat heavier single-headed beater will generally prove superior.

The Stroke

The proper bass drum stroke is achieved by striking the head with a direct, horizontal blow, immediately bringing the beater back to its starting position. Be sure to contact the drum half-way between the center and the edge to obtain the fullest sound.

THE CYMBALS

Hand Cymbals

For medium and large size bands, a matched pair of cymbals 16" to 18" in diameter will be most satisfactory.

Leather straps with leather or lamb's wool disks are the most popular devices for holding cymbals. Wooden handles are not recommended, since they will deaden the tone and may cause the cymbals to crack.

Playing the Cymbals

The cymbals are brought together with a glancing blow. The left hand (for a right-handed player) remains stationary, while the right hand executes the stroke. In concert situations, this action is repeated for successive blows.

In the marching band, it's sometimes acceptable to use an alternating up and down motion to minimize fatigue.

To muffle (or choke) the cymbals and stop the vibrations, the player draws the cymbals against the chest or forearms.

Cymbal knots should be tied correctly and checked frequently. Tie it again (directly on top of the first knot) for added security.

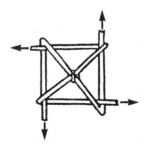

ELEMENTS OF MUSIC

Whole—Half—Quarter Notes

The duration of musical sounds (long or short) is indicated by different types of notes.

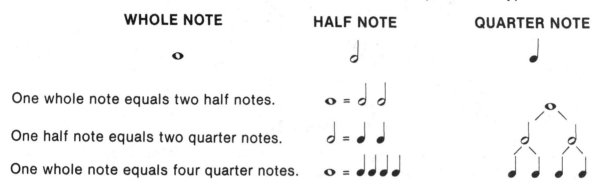

WHOLE NOTE	HALF NOTE	QUARTER NOTE

One whole note equals two half notes.

One half note equals two quarter notes.

One whole note equals four quarter notes.

Measure—Bar Lines—Double Bar Lines

Music is divided into equal parts called **MEASURES**.

BAR LINES indicate the beginning and end of measures.

DOUBLE BAR LINES, one thin and one thick, show the end of a piece.

Time Signatures and Note Values

TIME SIGNATURES are placed at the beginning of a piece of music. They contain two numbers that show the number of beats (or counts) in each measure and the kind of note that receives one beat.

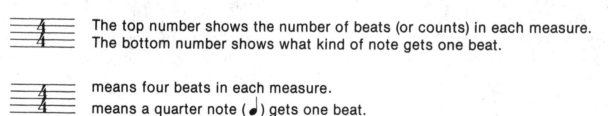

The top number shows the number of beats (or counts) in each measure.
The bottom number shows what kind of note gets one beat.

means four beats in each measure.
means a quarter note (♩) gets one beat.

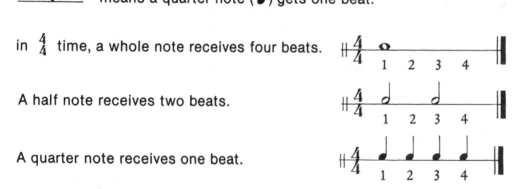

in 4/4 time, a whole note receives four beats.

A half note receives two beats.

A quarter note receives one beat.

At the beginning of each line of music there is a clef sign. Unpitched percussion music uses the neutral (ǂ) clef.

METRONOME—A device which produces clicks and/or light flashes to indicate the tempo of the music. For instance, ♩ = 120 means that the metronome will click 120 times in a minute and each click will, in this case, represent a quarter note.

TEMPO—The rate of speed of a musical piece or passage. Tempo may be indicated by a musical term, or by an exact metronome marking.

YOU ARE NOW READY TO PLAY

Things to remember:

Time Signatures and Note Values

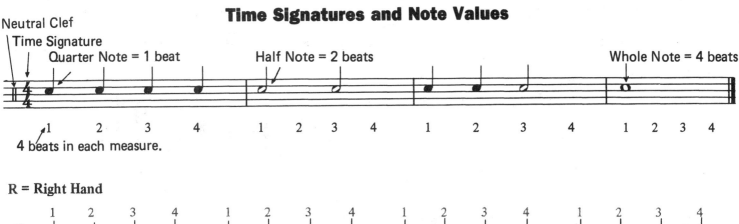

4 beats in each measure.

R = Right Hand

L = Left Hand

When alternating strokes, be sure to bring the left stick tip up as the right hand comes down, and the right stick tip up as the left hand comes down.

Repeat Signs

Two dots placed before a double bar line ⦂‖ means go back to the beginning and play again.

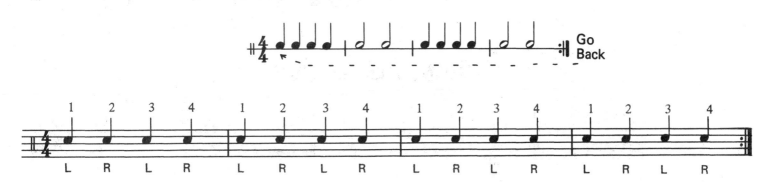

Some music in this method will contain Snare Drum and Bass Drum parts. It is suggested that each student practice both parts and develop the techniques of each instrument. The two parts may be played by one player, executing the bass drum part with the toe of his/her right foot as one would when playing at the drum set. The two parts may also be played as a duet by a snare drummer and bass drummer.

LESSON 1
Quarter Notes, Quarter Rests

COMBINATION STUDY

*Throughout this method all exercises should be practiced beginning with both the right hand and the left hand.

LESSON 2
Eighth Notes, Quarter Notes

An **EIGHTH NOTE** looks like a quarter note with a flag added to its stem: ♪

Two or more **EIGHTH NOTES** are joined together by a beam: ♫

COMBINATION STUDY

* 𝅗𝅥 =half note = two beats

LESSON 3
Quarter Notes, Quarter Rests, Eighth Notes

COMBINATION STUDY

* ▬ - half rest = two beats of silence

Dynamics

Dynamic signs indicate how loudly or softly music should be played.

The symbol f forte—means: loud

The symbol p piano—means: soft

A crescendo ⟨———— means: gradually get louder

A decrescendo ————⟩ means: gradually get softer

% = *repeat previous measure*

▬ = *whole rest* = 4 beats of silence

First and Second Endings

The repeat sign tells you to go back to the beginning. On the repeat, skip the first ending and play the second ending.

SOLO #1

* ✗ = play on rim

7/2/12

LESSON 4
Eighth Notes, Quarter Notes, Eighth Rests

𝄾 = eighth rest

COMBINATION STUDY

LESSON 5
Eighth Notes, Eighth Rests

7/2/12

COMBINATION STUDY

7/2/12

LESSON 6
Dotted Half Notes, Dotted Quarter Notes

A dot (•) placed after a note increases its value by one-half the value of the original note.

COMBINATION STUDY

8/28/12

SOLO #2

7/2/12

The symbol *ff* **fortissimo**—means: very loud
The symbol *pp* **pianissimo**—means: very soft

D.S. = **Dal Segno**—means: go back to the sign (𝄋)
Fine = the end
If we put them together, we get:
D.S. al Fine = Go back to the sign (𝄋) and play to the end, indicated by **Fine.**

* Repeats are traditionally not observed on a D.S.

7/2/12 8/28/1~ (AROUND KIT)

LESSON 7
Sixteenth Notes, Eighth Notes, Quarter Notes

A **sixteenth note** looks like an eighth note with a second flag added to its stem:

Two or more **sixteenth notes** are joined together by two beams.

LESSON 8
Sixteenth Notes, Eighth Notes

COMBINATION STUDY

1 + 2 +a 3 e + 4 +   1 +a 2 +a 3 e + 4 e +   1

SOLO #3

> = **Accent**—means: play the note a little louder
The symbol *mp* ***mezzo piano***—means: moderately soft
The symbol *mf* ***mezzo forte***—means: moderately loud

f-p = play *f* the first time, *p* on the repeat.

LESSON 9
Sixteenth Notes, Eighth Notes, Eighth Rests

9/11/12

COMBINATION STUDY

LESSON 10
Sixteenth Notes, Sixteenth Rests

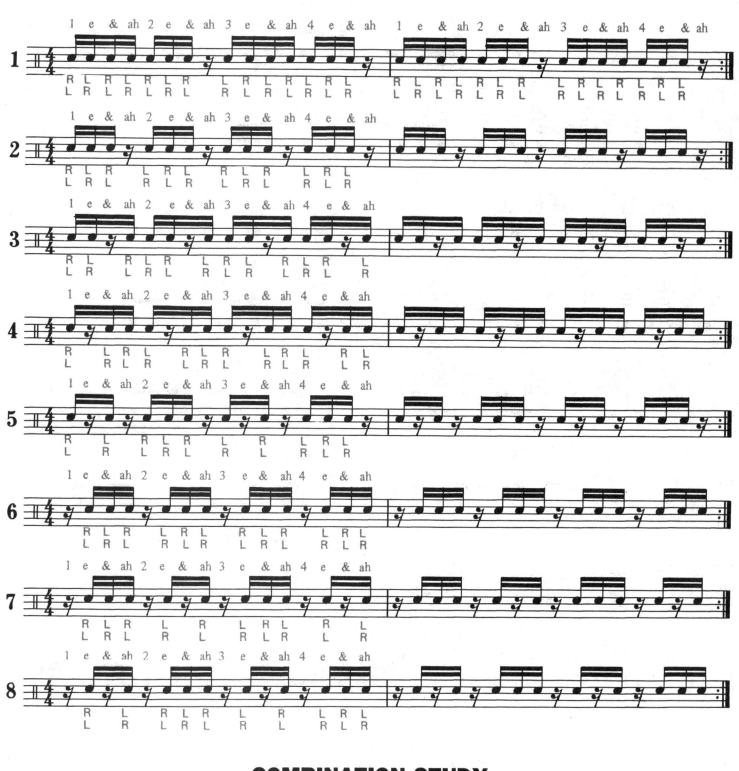

COMBINATION STUDY

SOLO #4

D.C. = **Da Capo**—means: go back to the beginning. Sometimes a composition ends with a separate closing section. This is called a *Coda* and is indicated by a Coda sign (⊕).

If we combine Coda with D.C., we get:
D.C. al Coda = Go back to the beginning and play to the Coda sign (⊕), then skip to the Coda to end the piece.

⊞ = repeat the previous two measures.

LESSON 11
Dotted Eighth and Sixteenth Notes

A dot (·) placed after a note increases its value by one-half the value of the original note.

Example:

COMBINATION STUDY

SOLO #5

LESSON 12
2/4 Time

The top number shows the number of beats (or counts) in each measure.
The bottom number shows what kind of note gets one beat.

means two beats in each measure.
means quarter note gets one beat.

COMBINATION STUDY

SOLO #6

* R.S. = rimshot: Place the tip of one stick on the drum head. Strike that stick in the middle with the other stick.

LESSON 13
Eighth Notes, Sixteenth Notes, Eighth Rests

COMBINATION STUDY

W/ B. Drums on 1,2 SNARE 1st 10/30/12
Go Around 10/23/12
KIT 11/6/12

LESSON 14
Sixteenth Notes, Sixteenth Rests

COMBINATION STUDY

SOLO #7

SOLO #8

LESSON 15
3/4 Time

In 3/4 time there are 3 beats in each measure and a quarter note receives one beat.

$\frac{3}{4}$ means three beats in each measure.
$\frac{3}{4}$ means quarter note gets one beat.

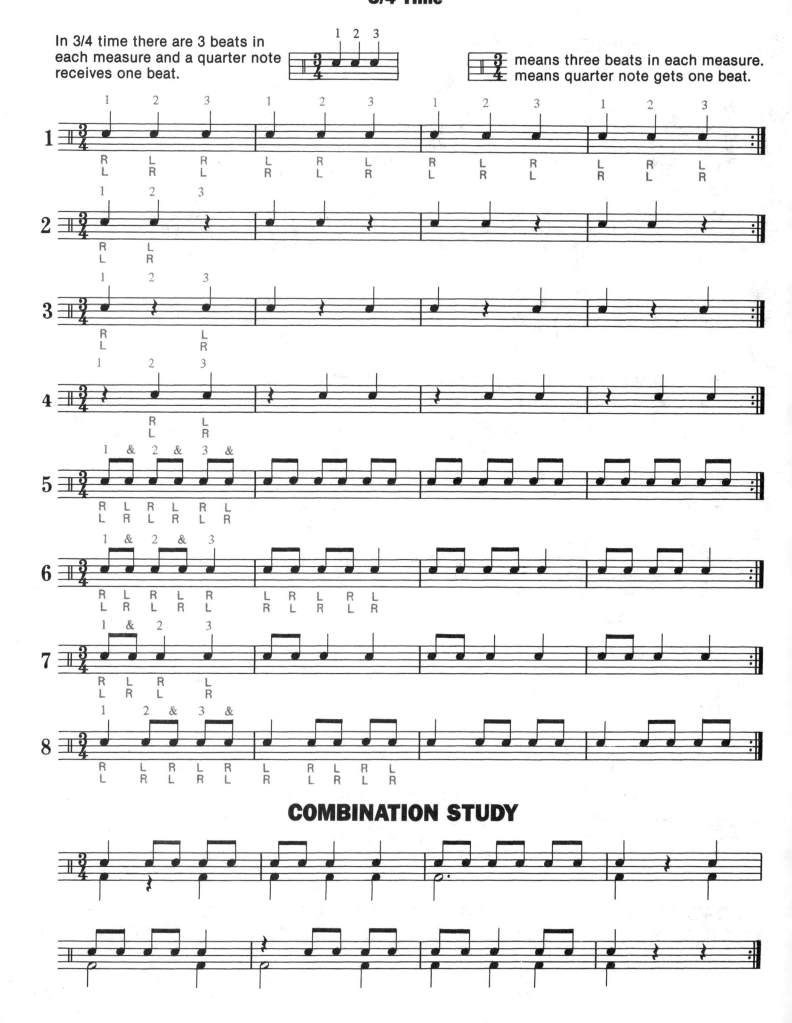

COMBINATION STUDY

LESSON 16
Sixteenth Notes, Eighth Notes

COMBINATION STUDY

SOLO #9

LESSON 17
The Roll

There are two types of rolls used by snare drummers: the double stroke and the multiple bounce or "buzz" roll. Rolls are indicated by three diagonal lines drawn through the stems of a note.

Example:

The double stroke roll, most commonly used by marching bands, is executed by playing two strokes with each hand. The first stroke (primary stroke) is executed by the wrist, while the second (secondary stroke) is a bounce produced by using the fingers. Both must be controlled and of equal volume.

The multiple bounce or unmeasured roll which is most often used by concert and drum-set drummers, is comprised of multiple bounces on each stick—often as many as 5–9 per stroke. In order to produce an even multiple bounce roll, make sure that each stick strikes the head in the same manner to achieve matching sounds. With time and practice the student will be able to develop a smooth and sustained multiple bounce roll.

It is possible to use multiple bounce rolls in all situations, including the Sousa marches on the following pages. Your teacher will show you how to use this technique.

LESSON 18
The 5-Stroke Roll

The 5-stroke roll consists of a series of 2 double strokes followed by a single stroke: Example: RRLLR or LLRRL. (At slow speeds, the strokes are executed individually.)

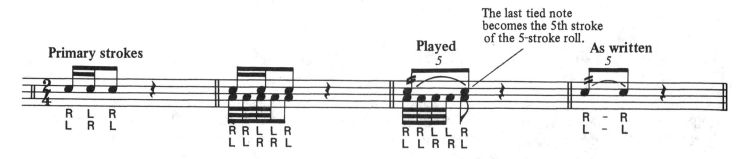

When playing 5-stroke rolls, the hand that begins the roll will also end it.

COMBINATION STUDY

SOLO #10

2/19/13, 1/15/13, 11/27/12

2/19/13   3/19/13

LESSON 19
The 9-Stroke Roll

The 9-stroke roll consists of a series of 4 double strokes followed by a single stroke.
Example: RRLLRRLLR or LLRRLLRRL. (At slow speeds, the strokes are executed individually.)

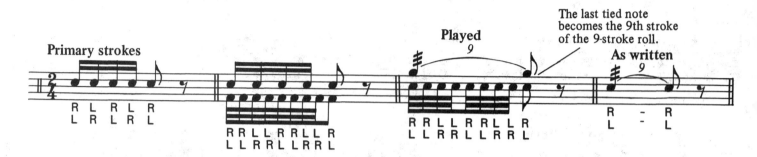

When playing 9-stroke rolls, the hand that begins the roll will also end it.

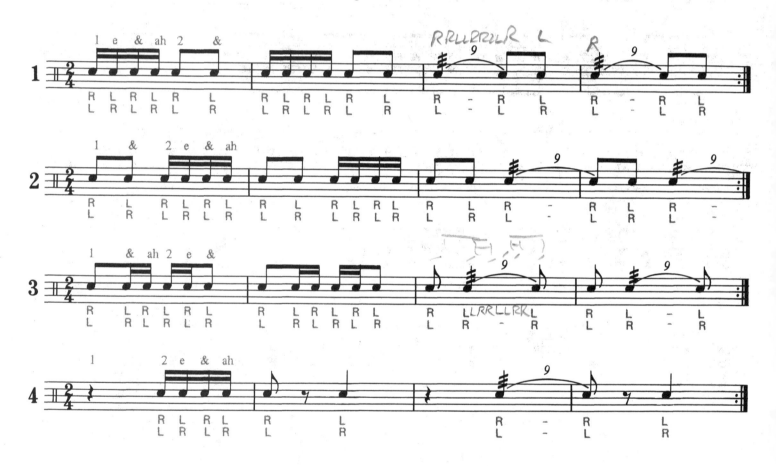

COMBINATION STUDY

SOLO #11

SOLO #12

LESSON 20
The 13-Stroke Roll

The 13-stroke roll consists of a series of 6 double strokes followed by a single stroke.
Example: RRLLRRLLRRLLR or LLRRLLRRLLRRL. (At slow speeds, the strokes are executed individually.)

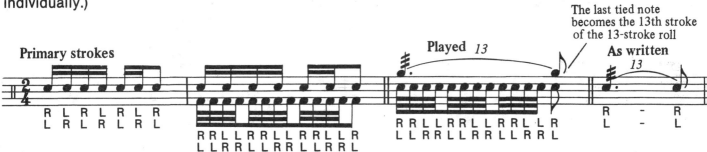

When playing 13-stroke rolls, the hand that begins the roll will also end it.

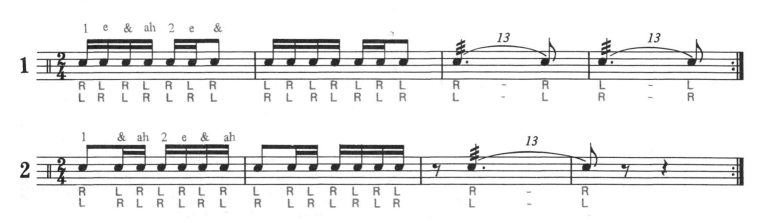

The 17-Stroke Roll

The 17-stroke roll consists of 8 double strokes followed by a single stroke.
Example: RRLLRRLLRRLLRRLLR or LLRRLLRRLLRRLLRRL. (At slow speeds, the strokes are executed individually.)

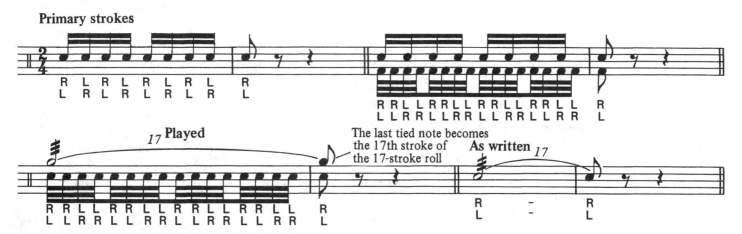

When playing 17-stroke rolls, the hand that begins the roll will also end it.

SOLO #13

THE U.S. FIELD ARTILLERY MARCH

SOUSA
Arr. Feldstein/Black

5/27/14

LESSON 21
3/4 Time, Rolls

COMBINATION STUDY

SOLO #14

10/80/12 ON SNARE ON KIT w/ 2,4 HI HAT
w/ 4 BEATS N
ON B.D.
w/

LESSON 22
Triplets

A triplet is a group of three notes of equal value, usually played in the place of one note. A triplet will have the numeral "3" placed above or beneath the center note.

COMBINATION STUDY

LESSON 23
Sixteenth-Note Triplets, Eighth Notes

COMBINATION STUDY

SOLO #15

LESSON 24
The 7-Stroke Roll

Because the 7-stroke roll starts and ends on opposite hands, it is usually not alternated as were the 5, 9, 13 and 17-stroke rolls. It most often begins with the left hand and ends with the right and is frequently used as a substitute for the 5-stroke roll.

COMBINATION STUDY

SOLO #16

LESSON 25
Alla Breve or "Cut-Time"

The time signature for Alla Breve (cut time) is $\frac{2}{2}$ or ₵. There are two beats or counts in each measure of cut time and a half note receives one beat or count.

Example: ₵ or $\frac{2}{2}$ = Beats (or Counts) in each measure.

₵ or $\frac{2}{2}$ = (Half) note or rest receives one beat (or Count).

LESSON 26
Eighth Notes, Quarter Notes

COMBINATION STUDY

SOLO #17

HANDS ACROSS THE SEA

SOUSA
Arr. Feldstein/Black

*Play the 2nd & 4th quarter notes a little louder than the 1st & 3rd.

LESSON 27

The Flam

The flam is a combination of a small note (grace note) and a main note. Its purpose is to produce a broader sound (tenuto). The sticks do not strike the head at the same time, but must strike close enough so that they will almost sound as one stroke. If the grace note is played by the left hand, the main note is played by the right and vice versa. The name of the flam is designated according to the hand that strikes the main note.

The flam is not necessarily an accented note and should be played at a normal volume unless the main note is accompanied by an accent.

Example:

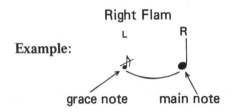

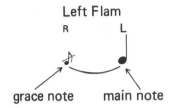

Position for right-hand flam.

Position for left-hand flam.

The hand playing the grace note starts approximately two inches above the head. After playing the grace note, the stick moves to the up position. The stick playing the main note rebounds to approximately two inches above the head, ready to play the grace note of the next flam.

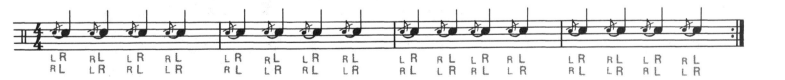

LESSON 27
(Continued)

COMBINATION STUDY

SOLO #18

open / closed   10/8/13

Moderato ♩= 112

6/3/14

LESSON 28
Flam Rudiments

Flam Accent
(also called Flam Accent No. 1)

A flam accent combines a flam with two other single strokes. Flam accents are played alternately.

1

Flam Tap

A flam tap is a flam combined with a second stroke, making one group of double strokes.

2

Flamacue

A flamacue is a combination of two flams and single strokes with an accent placed on the second note.

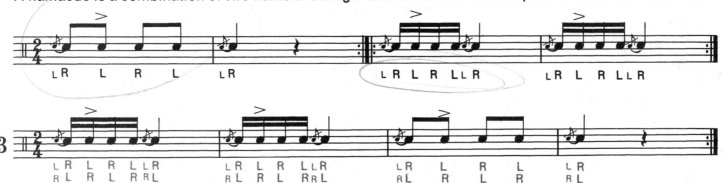

3

COMBINATION STUDY

(Flam tap)   (Flamacue)   (Flam tap)

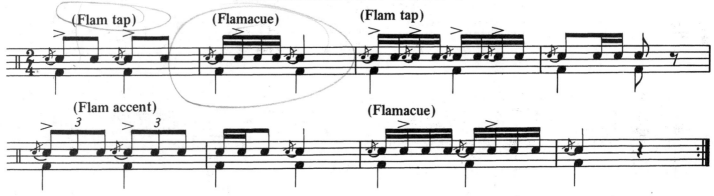

(Flam accent)   (Flamacue)

SOLO #19

*Use Flam Tap, Flamacue & Flam Accent stickings where possible.

THE THUNDERER

$\frac{2}{\text{—}}$ = rest for two measures

SOUSA
Arr. Feldstein/Black

*This roll is often played as a 7 stroke roll to add excitment to the end of the piece.

LESSON 29
6/8 Time

In 6/8 time there are six beats in each measure and an eighth note receives one beat.

6 means six beats in each measure.
8 means an eighth note gets one beat.

COMBINATION STUDY

(Flam Accent) (Flam Tap)

(Flam Accent)

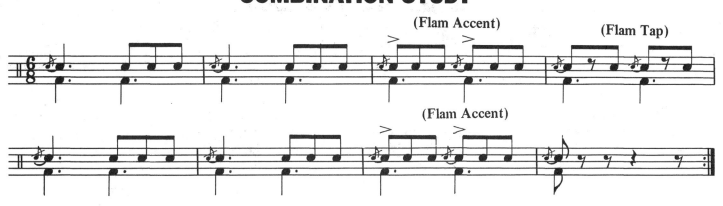

LESSON 30
Eighth Notes, Sixteenth Notes, Eighth Rests

COMBINATION STUDY

LESSON 31
Rolls in 6/8

The 5-Stroke Roll

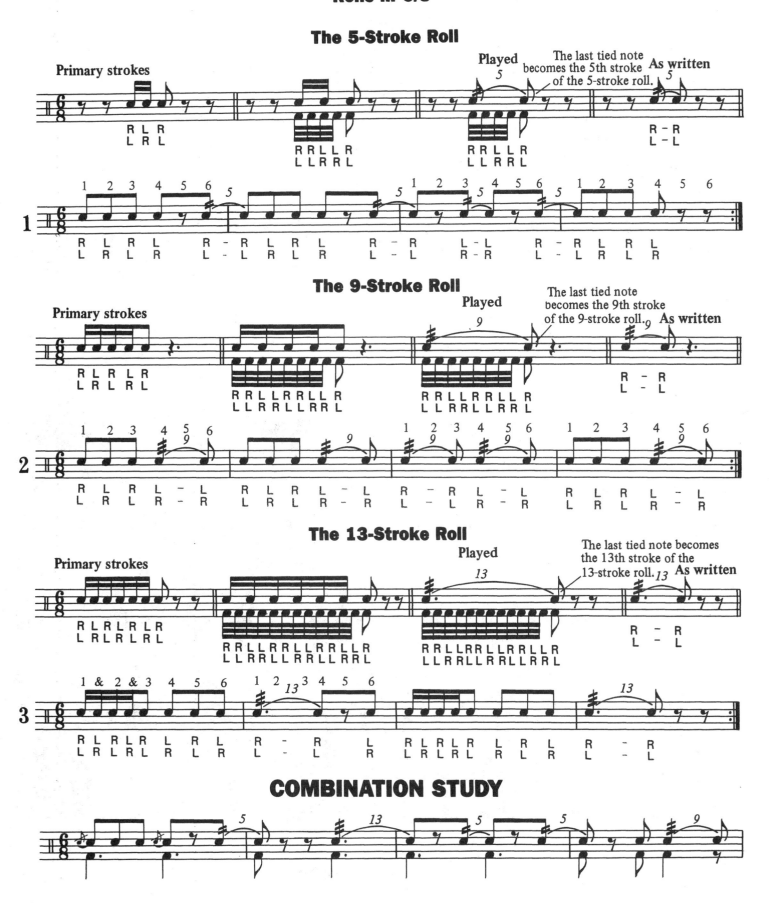

The 9-Stroke Roll

The 13-Stroke Roll

COMBINATION STUDY

SOLO #20

*Use Flam Accent and Flam Tap stickings where possible.

LESSON 32
6/8 "in 2"

When 6/8 time is played at fast
tempos, it is usually counted "in 2".

COMBINATION STUDY

(Flam Accent) (Flam Tap)
"In 2"

LESSON 33
6/8 "in 2" with Rolls

When 6/8 is played "in 2", the primary strokes of the rolls become eighth notes.

COMBINATION STUDY

THE LIBERTY BELL

SOUSA
Arr. Feldstein/Black

*Play 1st & 2nd endings on D.S.

8/26/14

LESSON 34
The Drag
(sometimes referred to as a 3-stroke ruff)

The drag (or 3-stroke ruff) consists of two grace notes and a main note. The two grace notes are played softer than the main note. The drag may begin with either hand.

The 3-Stroke Ruff

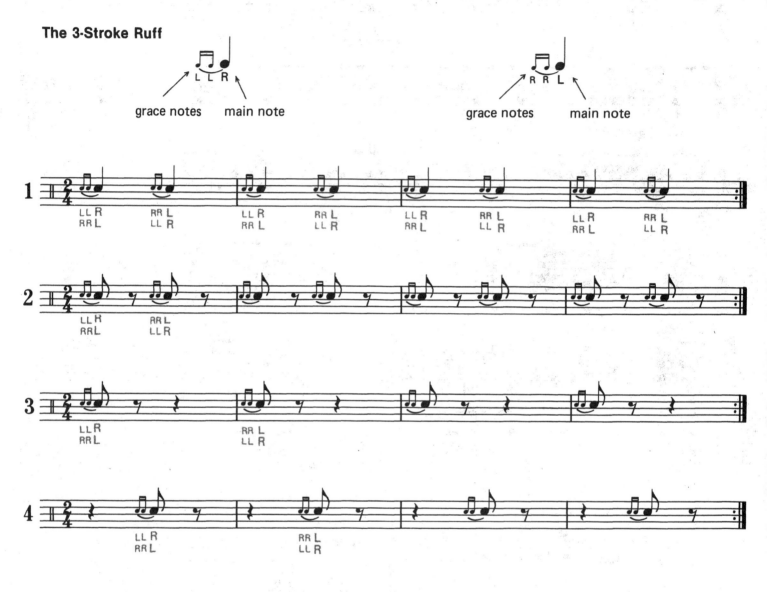

COMBINATION STUDY

LESSON 35
The Ruff

A ruff is a combination of two or more grace notes and a main note. The grace notes are played softer than the main note. The ruff may begin with either hand.

The 4-Stroke Ruff

The 4-stroke ruff consists of three grace notes and a main note. The 4-stroke ruff is played with single strokes rather than bounces and may begin with either hand.

COMBINATION STUDY

SOLO #21

LESSON 36
Syncopation

Syncopation occurs when a temporary displacement of the regular metrical accent occurs, causing the emphasis to shift from a strong accent to a weak accent.

COMBINATION STUDY

LESSON 37
Syncopation in 3/4 Time, 2/4 Time

COMBINATION STUDY

SOLO #22

D.S. = **Dal Segno**—means: go back to the sign (𝄋)
Sometimes a composition ends with a separate
closing section. This is called a *Coda* and is
indicated by a *Coda* sign (⊕).

If we combine *Coda* with *D.S.*, we get:
D.S. al Coda = Go back to the sign (𝄋) and play to
the *Coda* sign (⊕), then skip to the *Coda* to end the
piece.

LESSON 38
Tied Notes

A curved line is sometimes used to connect two notes which appear on the same line or space. This is called a tie. The first note is played, while the time value of the second note is added to the first note.

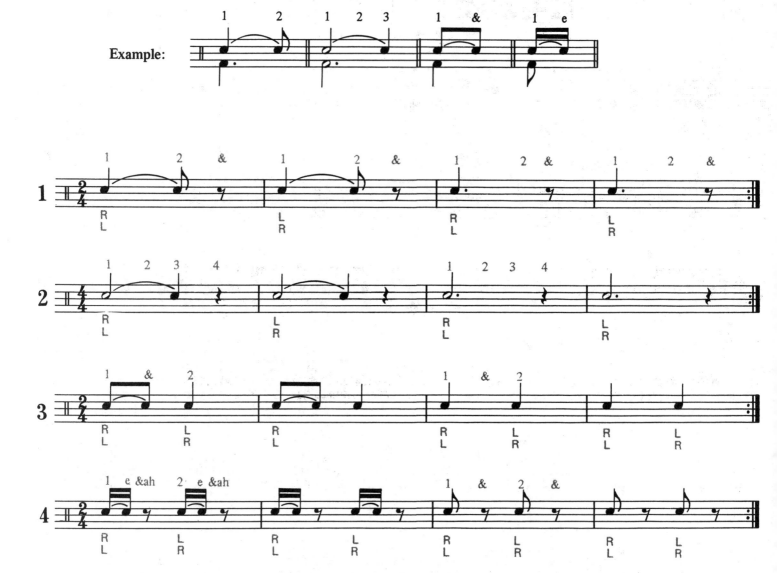

COMBINATION STUDY

LESSON 39
Tied Notes, Rolls

COMBINATION STUDY

SOLO #23

THE STARS AND STRIPES FOREVER

SOUSA
Arr. Feldstein/Black

Moderato ♩ = 116-120

*Play as 7 stroke rolls on repeat

82

SOLO #24

// = Grand Pause (G.P.): A break or
extended rest in music.

*S.S. = stick shot: Place the tip of one stick on the drum head. Strike that stick in the middle with the other stick.

LESSON 40
The Alternate 7-Stroke Roll

Up until now we have played the 7-stroke roll based on a triplet feel. The 7-stroke roll may also be played based on a sixteenth-note feel.

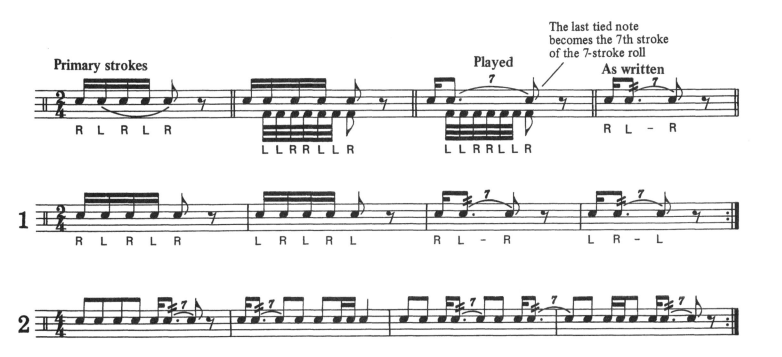

COMBINATION STUDY

SOLO #25

LESSON 41

STREET BEAT #1

STREET BEAT #2

STREET BEAT #3

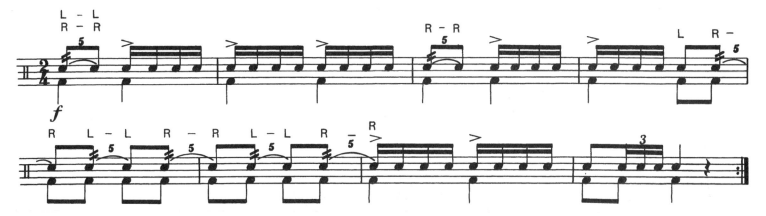

STREET BEAT #4

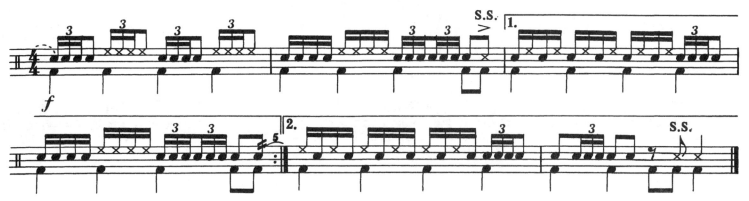

SOLO #26

This page has been left blank to facilitate page turns.

DUET #1

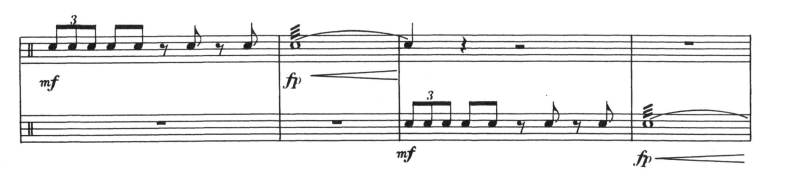

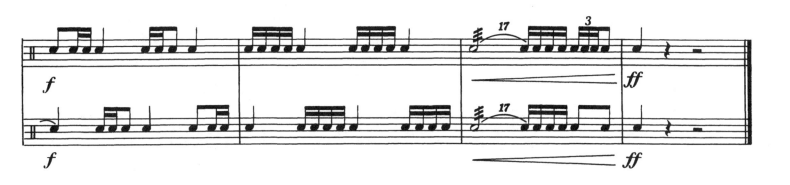

LESSON 42
The Single Paradiddle

The single paradiddle is a combination of two single strokes and one group of double strokes, with an accent on the first note. It is most often played in an alternating manner.

The single paradiddle may also be practiced with various accent placements.

The Double Paradiddle

The double paradiddle consists of two sets of singles and one set of doubles, with an accent on the first note.

The double paradiddle may also be practiced with various accent placements.

The Triple Paradiddle

The triple paradiddle consists of three sets of singles and one set of doubles, with an accent on the first note. Additional accents may be added.

The triple paradiddle may also be practiced with various accent placements.

COMBINATION STUDY

*The accents below indicate single, double and triple paradiddles.

SOLO #27

Andante ♩ = 104

* Watch carefully! This solo contains concealed single, double and triple paradiddles.

LESSON 43

The Flam Paradiddle

The flam paradiddle combines a flam with a single stroke and one group of double strokes.

COMBINATION STUDY

SOLO #28

LESSON 44

Drag Paradiddle #1

The drag paradiddle #1 is formed by a tap, followed by two grace notes in front of a single paradiddle.

Drag Paradiddle #2

The drag paradiddle #2 is formed by a tap, followed by two sets of grace notes in front of a single paradiddle.

COMBINATION STUDY

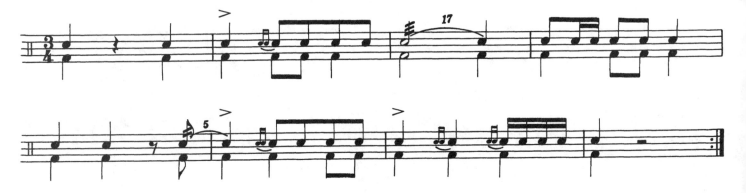

LESSON 45
Lesson 25

1. *Lesson 25* is a combination of a drag and two single strokes in a different rhythmic pattern.

2. *Lesson 25* may also be played in an inverted form by starting on the eighth note rather than on the drag.

COMBINATION STUDY

SOLO #29

LESSON 46

The Single Ratamacue

The single ratamacue is a combination of a drag followed by three single strokes, usually ending with an accent.

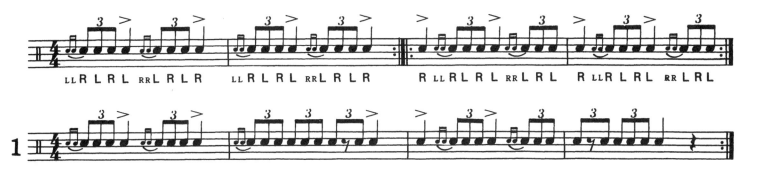

The Double Ratamacue

A double ratamacue consists of a drag followed by a single ratamacue.

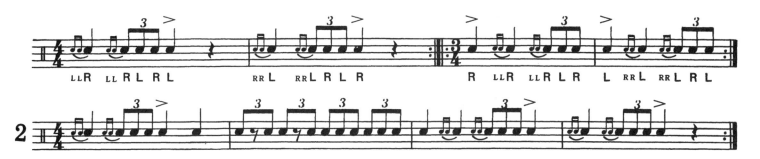

The Triple Ratamacue

A triple ratamacue consists of two drags followed by a single ratamacue.

COMBINATION STUDY

SOLO #30

Moderato ♩ = 120

LESSON 47

The Paradiddle-Diddle

A paradiddle-diddle is formed by adding double strokes to the end of a paradiddle.

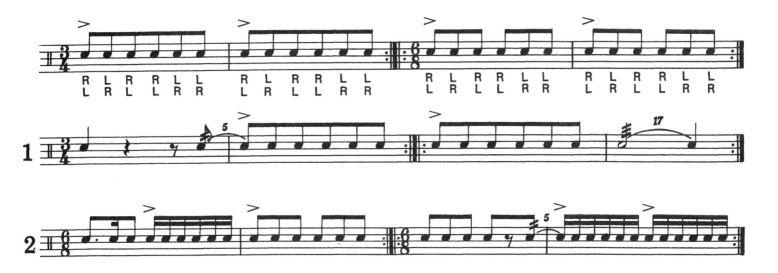

The Flam Paradiddle-Diddle

A flam paradiddle-diddle is formed by adding double strokes to the end of a flam paradiddle.

COMBINATION STUDY

SOLO #31

Moderato ♩. = 112

DUET #2

V.S. = *Volti Subito*—means: turn the page *quickly.*

V.S.

LESSON 48

INTRODUCTION TO THE ORCHESTRAL STYLE OF DRUMMING

This section is designed to prepare the percussionist to play in a concert situation.

It's the authors' objective to assist the student in achieving a feeling of confidence with orchestral percussion music. Toward that aim, we have included selections written in orchestral style, along with accessory techniques, multiple percussion solos and orchestral excerpts.

Remember that in ensemble playing technique alone is not of prime importance; of equal or greater importance is how that single part was conceived by the composer to fit into the ensemble as a whole.

The Multiple Bounce/Orchestral Roll

The multiple bounce roll commonly used by concert and drum-set players is comprised of as many as 5 to 9 bounces per hand. The exact number varies according to the tempo of the music, as well as the technical ability of the player. It's extremely important that each stick strike the head from the same angle and height.

Development of the Multiple Bounce Roll

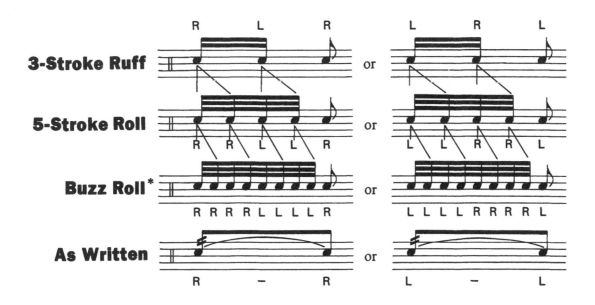

*The multiple bounce or "buzz" roll may sometimes be notated ♪.

LESSON 48
(continued)

Use multiple bounce rolls throughout unless otherwise indicated.

COMBINATION STUDY

SOLO #32
A-B-A Form

Music, like speech, is organized into a variety of thoughts (sections) and **A-B-A** form is one of the most common ways of organizing musical thoughts. The **A** section presents the first musical idea; it is followed by a contrasting **B** section and then the **A** section returns again, although this time the **A** section may be slightly altered. The following solo is in **A-B-A** form.

LESSON 49

5/4 Time

In 5/4 time there are five beats in each measure and a quarter note receives one beat.

means five beats in each measure.
means quarter note gets one beat.

5/4 time with a feeling of 3/4 plus 2/4

5/4 time with a feeling of 2/4 plus 3/4

COMBINATION STUDY

LESSON 50
7/4 Time

In 7/4 time there are seven beats in each measure and a quarter note receives one beat.

means seven beats in each measure.
means quarter note gets one beat.

7/4 time with a feeling of 4/4 plus 3/4

7/4 time with a feeling of 3/4 plus 4/4

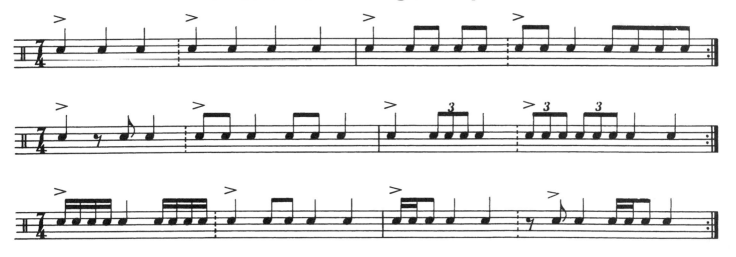

COMBINATION STUDY

LESSON 51

Combining "like times" with a common denominator of four

COMBINATION STUDY

SOLO #33

LESSON 52

3/8 Time

In 3/8 time there are three beats in each measure and an eighth note receives one beat.

means three beats in each measure.
means an eighth note gets one beat.

COMBINATION STUDY

5/8 Time

In 5/8 time there are five beats in each measure and an eighth note receives one beat.

means five beats in each measure.
means an eighth note gets one beat.

COMBINATION STUDY

LESSON 53

9/8 Time

In 9/8 time there are nine beats in each measure and an eighth note receives one beat.

9/8 means nine beats in a measure.
means an eighth note gets one beat.

COMBINATION STUDY

12/8 Time

In 12/8 time there are 12 beats in each measure and an eighth note receives one beat.

12/8 means 12 beats in each measure.
means an eighth note gets one beat.

COMBINATION STUDY

LESSON 54
Combining "like times" with a common denominator of eight

COMBINATION STUDY

SOLO #34

Theme and Variations

Another popular form is called the THEME AND VARIATIONS. In this case, the A theme is followed by a number of variations, each assigned its own letter designation. Therefore, a Theme with Variations might be described as **A-B-C-D-E**, etc., or THEME followed by VARIATION I, VARIATION II, VARIATION III, VARIATION IV, etc.

LESSON 55
Combining denominators of four and eight

♪ = ♪ indicates that the speed of the eighth note remains consistent when changing meters.

COMBINATION STUDY

SOLO #35

DUET #3

Excerpts From Actual Band Pieces

TEMPLE HILL
An American Essay for Band

John O'Reilly

MOUNTAIN MAJESTY

Sandy Feldstein

LESSON 56
Multiple Percussion Concepts

Multiple percussion playing involves one person playing a combination of various percussion instruments.

On this page we combine the snare drum with a tom-tom. First, play the solo with sticks, then play it again using hard timpani or yarn marimba mallets. Choose the mallets whose sound you feel best fits the solo.

Mallet choice will depend upon the type of drums used and, if not specified by the composer, is left to the discretion of the performer. As stated previously, the final decision should be based on the quality of sound desired.

Suggested Set-Up:

* Double stop: Two notes played simultaneously.

The solos and exercises on the following pages are designed to help make the percussion student more aware of the variety of tonal possibilities available from percussion instruments, and to develop the necessary techniques for reading multiple percussion music.

LESSON 57
Tonal Properties of the Snare Drum

Various areas of the drum produce different tones. The following solo explores the various colors available.

1. Edge of the Head
2. Halfway or Middle of the Head
3. Center of the Head

SOLO #36

LESSON 58
Two-Hand Independence

Snare drum music is sometimes written so that each hand may play independently. In the following exercises the right hand will play the higher notes, while the left hand will play the lower notes.

COMBINATION STUDY

SOLO #37

A trap table (covered with soft material) placed next to the performer will aid in the execution of quiet stick and mallet changes.

Suggested Set-Up:

LESSON 59
Quarter-Note Triplets

A triplet is a group of three notes of equal value, usually played in the place of one note. A triplet will have the numeral "3" placed above or beneath the center note.

COMBINATION STUDY

SOLO #38

* You may wish to play this solo as a multiple percussion piece by playing the L.H. part on a tom-tom.

LESSON 60
Syncopation

Syncopation occurs when there is a temporary feeling of change from the regular meter, accent or rhythm.

COMBINATION STUDY

SOLO #39

* You may wish to play this solo as a multiple percussion piece by playing the L.H. part on a tom-tom.

Player 1 = Sn. Dr. and Tom-Tom
Player 2 = Sn. Dr.

DUET #4

* Player number two should turn the page.

LESSON 61
The Triangle

The triangle is generally used to add a touch of brilliance and color to music. It is made from a piece of steel or aluminum bent in a shape which allows it to be suspended from a metal clip. The triangle is usually played with a steel beater, although wood, plastic and other materials may be used to obtain additional sounds.

Performance Techniques

The triangle must be freely suspended—preferably from a piece of catgut (avoid string as it allows the triangle to turn while being played.) It may also be suspended from a piece of catgut attached to a metal clip.

The triangle may be struck in a variety of spots, including the bottom or the closed side.

Moderato

mf - f

The roll on the triangle is executed in a closed corner by alternating beater strokes against adjoining sides. When the triangle is suspended from two clips, the player may use a beater in each hand to produce the roll or to execute fast passages.

 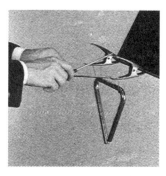

Allegro

f

To stop the triangle from ringing while holding it, bring the last three fingers into contact with the instrument. When the triangle is suspended from a clip, use the other hand to damp the vibrations.

Slowly

mf

* Accessory instruments may sometimes be written on a single line.

LESSON 62
The Suspended Cymbal

The suspended cymbal is capable of producing a variety of sounds depending upon size and weight of the cymbal, where it is struck and the type of sticks or mallets used. The following exercises should be played on suspended cymbal with a variety of mallets. Strike at the edge, bow (halfway between the edge and the bell) and the bell of the cymbal to obtain varied sounds.

Performance Techniques

Cymbal rolls are most often played on the suspended cymbal. All such rolls are executed with single strokes by striking opposite sides of the cymbal in an alternating manner. Depending upon the character of sound desired, the implements used vary from drum sticks to various marimba or timpani mallets. Experiment with a variety of mallets.

The larger a suspended cymbal, the slower it is to respond when struck. Because of this, most players "prime" the cymbal by tapping it lightly (and quietly) to set it into motion in anticipation of the written stroke. To muffle or damp the vibrations of the cymbal, grasp it with your hand(s) or use body pressure against the edge.

Rhythmic passages are best articulated by snare drum sticks playing near the edge. However, the cymbal may be struck anywhere from the edge to the center.

w/stick (damp on all rests)

LESSON 63
The Tambourine

The tambourine consists of a wooden, plastic or metal shell upon which is stretched a single head. (Rock and pop musicians sometimes use a tambourine without a head.) The shell contains numerous loosely mounted jingles which vibrate against one another when the drum head is struck.

Performance Techniques

The tambourine head may be struck by the finger tips (*p-mf*), knuckles or heel of hand (*mf-f*) or the flat of the hand (*f-ff*), depending upon the sound and volume level desired.

Moderato

For soft, rapid passages, the tambourine may be placed on a horizontal music stand (cushioned by a towel) and played with fingertips, sticks or mallets.

Moderato

Loud, rapid parts which are too difficult (rapid) to be executed by just one hand may be played by striking the tambourine alternately between a knee and a fist. Place one foot on a chair and hold the tambourine head downward while using the other fist to strike the inside of the head. Alternate the tambourine between the knee and the fist.

Presto

LESSON 64
Tambourine Rolls

There are two kinds of rolls used on the tambourine: the shake roll and the thumb roll. The "thumb roll" is ideal for rolls of short duration whereas the shake roll is best used for long and loud rolls.

The shake roll is achieved by holding the tambourine in the hand and rotating the wrist rapidly.

The thumb roll is achieved by pushing the end of the thumb around the circumference of the head at about an 80 degree angle from the surface, causing it to bounce or skip much as chalk will do on a blackboard. The friction between the stiff thumb and the head will cause the jingles to rattle. (It may be necessary to moisten the thumb.)

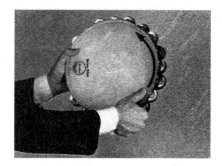

The Woodblock

The woodblock is made from hard wood carefully selected for its resonant tone. It is most commonly played with drum sticks (use tips for fast, articulate rhythms; butt end for isolated strokes) or rubber or plastic mallets. The woodblock may be mounted on a holder, held in the hand, or placed on a padded table.

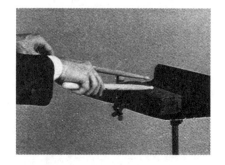

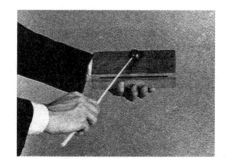

Excerpts From Actual Band Pieces

Practice each accessory part, then combine with other players if possible.

WOOD COUNTY CELEBRATION

John O'Reilly

AT END OF DAY

Brahms/Barnby
Arr. by Sandy Feldstein

CHANNEL ISLANDS OVERTURE

Sandy Feldstein

CHANNEL ISLANDS OVERTURE

(continued)

DUET #5
Snare Drum and Tambourine

12/10/13

LESSON 65
Corps-Style Rudiments

Rudimental snare drum solos have undergone many changes over the past several decades. Largely influenced by drum and bugle corps, today's rudimentalist has a new percussion vocabulary. Due to the new rudiment patterns (see P.A.S. International Drum Rudiments, pages 78-79) and various visual effects, the new rudimental solo has developed into a highly creative and interesting piece of music. Pay particular attention to sticking in order to play this idiom correctly. This section will introduce you to a number of corps-style rudiments.

The Swiss Army Triplet

The Swiss Army Triplet is a flam combined with two strokes.

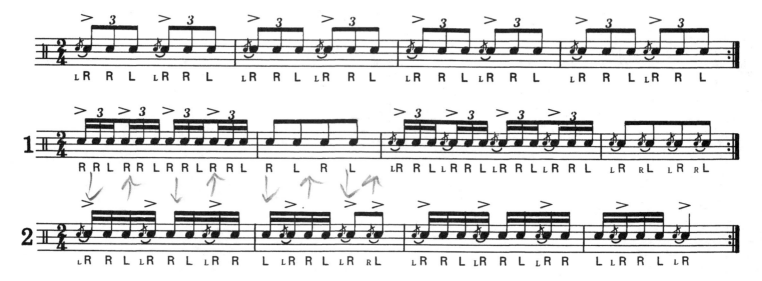

The Pataflafla

The pataflafla is a flam combined with two single strokes followed by a flam.

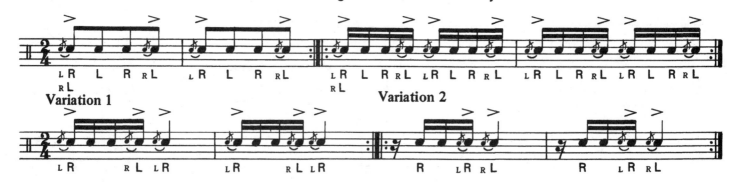

COMBINATION STUDY

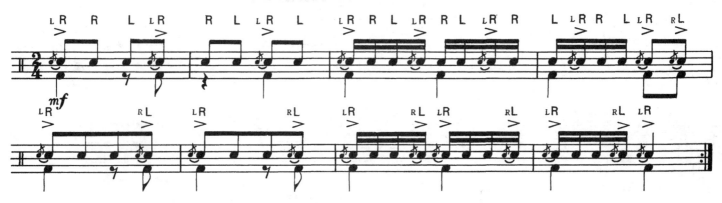

SOLO #40

Moderato ♩ = 112

Allegro ♩ = 132

* Rim Shot (RS) - Strike the drum so that the stick strikes the drum head and rim simultaneously.

LESSON 66
The 6-Stroke Roll

The 6-stroke roll consists of a tap followed by two double strokes and a tap.

Example: R LLRR L or L RRLL R

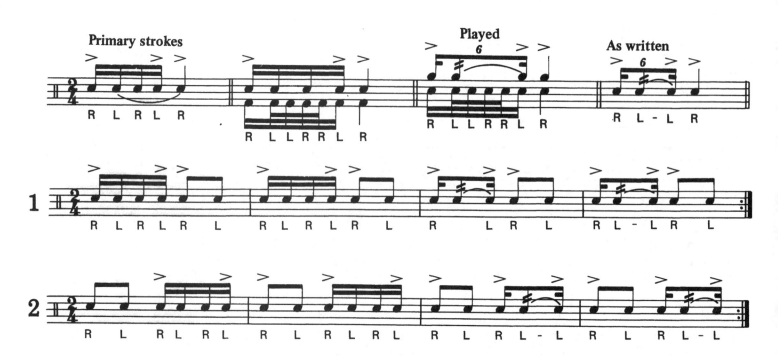

6-Stroke Roll Variations

COMBINATION STUDY

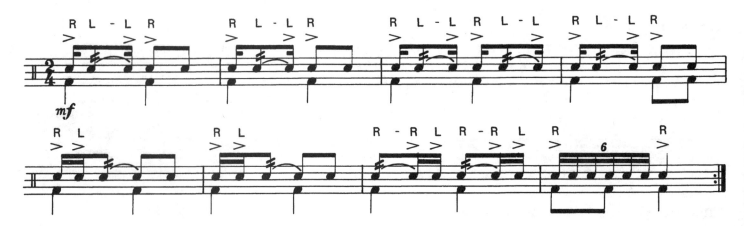

LESSON 67
The 10-Stroke Roll

The 10-stroke roll consists of a series of four double strokes followed by two single strokes.

Example: RRLLRRLLRL or LLRRLLRRLR. (At slow tempos, the strokes are executed individually.)

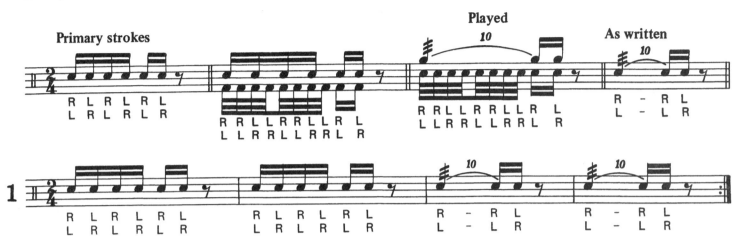

The 11-Stroke Roll

The 11-stroke roll consists of five double strokes followed by a single stroke.

Example: RRLLRRLLRRL or LLRRLLRRLLR. (At slow tempos, the strokes are executed individually.)

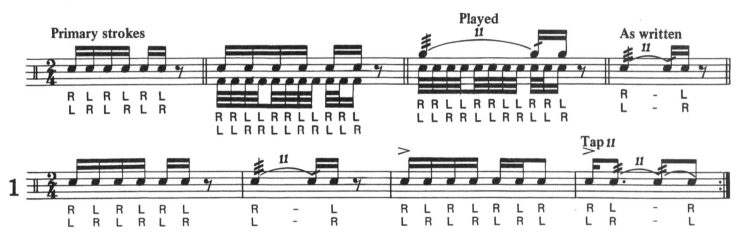

The 15-Stroke Roll

The 15-stroke roll consists of seven double strokes followed by a single stroke.

Example: RRLLRRLLRRLLRRL or LLRRLLRRLLRRLLR. (At slower tempos, the strokes are executed individually.)

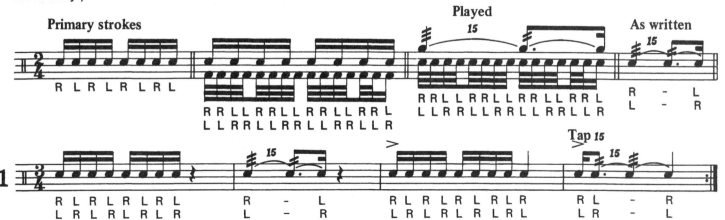

SOLO #41

LESSON 68

The Single Flammed Mill

The Single Flammed Mill is a double stroke, with the first note flammed, followed by two single strokes.

The Single Dragadiddle

The Single Dragadiddle is a double stroke followed by a tap, then by a double stroke.

The Flam Drag

The Flam Drag is a flam followed by a double stroke, then by a single stroke.

COMBINATION STUDY

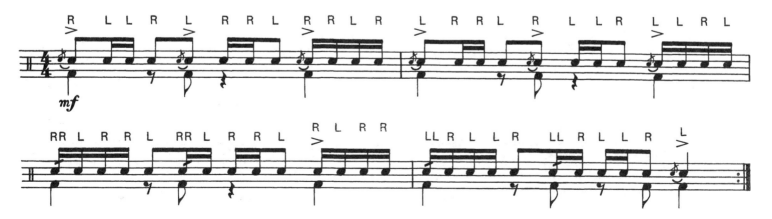

SOLO #42

LESSON 69

The Triple-Stroke Roll

The triple-stroke roll consists of three right strokes followed by three left strokes.

Back Sticking (B.S.)

Back sticking is accomplished by turning the drum stick so that the butt end strikes the drum head (each stick is simply rotated in a clockwise direction). Both matched and traditional snare drum grips can be used successfully when back sticking.

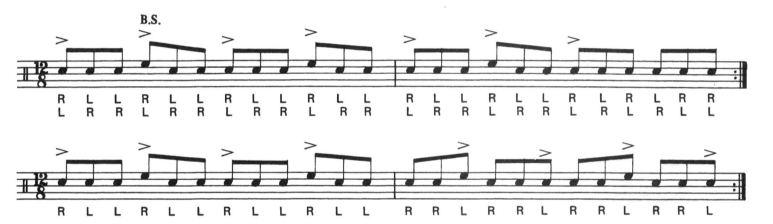

Tap Sticking (T.S.)

Tap sticking consists of striking the right stick on the left stick (R) or the left stick on the right stick (L) approximately four inches above the drum head.

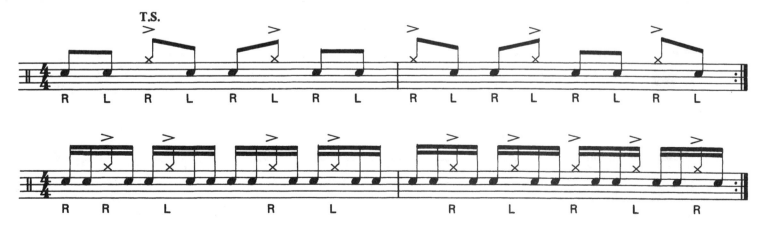

LESSON 70

Double Rim Shot (D.R.S.)

The double rim shot is performed by striking the drum so that both sticks simultaneously strike the head and rim.

Corps-Style Stick Shot (S.S.)

Stick shots are performed by striking the right stick on top of the left stick while the left stick is on the drum and rim simultaneously.

3:2 Ritumba Clave

Rim Click (R.C.)

The butt end of the left stick strikes the rim while the left palm holds the shoulder of the stick in the center of the drum.

SOLO #43

FINAL RUDIMENTAL SOLO

FINAL ORCHESTRAL SOLO

* Strike left stick with right stick.

FINAL MULTIPLE PERCUSSION SOLO

FINAL ORCHESTRAL DUET

1. Sn. Dr. and Tri.
2. Sn. Dr. and Wood Block

FINAL RUDIMENTAL DUET

PERCUSSIVE ARTS SOCIETY INTERNATIONAL DRUM RUDIMENTS

All rudiments should be practiced: *open* (slow) to *close* (fast) to *open* (slow) and/or at an even moderate march tempo.

I. ROLL RUDIMENTS

A. SINGLE STROKE ROLL RUDIMENTS

1. SINGLE STROKE ROLL *

2. SINGLE STROKE FOUR

3. SINGLE STROKE SEVEN

B. MULTIPLE BOUNCE ROLL RUDIMENTS

4. MULTIPLE BOUNCE ROLL

5. TRIPLE STROKE ROLL

C. DOUBLE STROKE OPEN ROLL RUDIMENTS

6. DOUBLE STROKE OPEN ROLL *

7. FIVE STROKE ROLL *

8. SIX STROKE ROLL

9. SEVEN STROKE ROLL *

10. NINE STROKE ROLL *

11. TEN STROKE ROLL *

12. ELEVEN STROKE ROLL *

13. THIRTEEN STROKE ROLL *

14. FIFTEEN STROKE ROLL *

15. SEVENTEEN STROKE ROLL

II. DIDDLE RUDIMENTS

16. SINGLE PARADIDDLE *

17. DOUBLE PARADIDDLE*

18. TRIPLE PARADIDDLE

19. SINGLE PARADIDDLE-DIDDLE

*These rudiments are also included in the original Standard 26 American Drum Rudiments.

III. FLAM RUDIMENTS

20. FLAM *

21. FLAM ACCENT *

22. FLAM TAP *

23. FLAMACUE *

24. FLAM PARADIDDLE *

25. SINGLE FLAMMED MILL

26. FLAM PARADIDDLE-DIDDLE *

27. PATAFLAFLA

28. SWISS ARMY TRIPLET

29. INVERTED FLAM TAP

30. FLAM DRAG

IV. DRAG RUDIMENTS

31. DRAG *

32. SINGLE DRAG TAP *

33. DOUBLE DRAG TAP *

34. LESSON 25 *

35. SINGLE DRAGADIDDLE

36. DRAG PARADIDDLE #1*

37. DRAG PARADIDDLE #2 *

38. SINGLE RATAMACUE *

39. DOUBLE RATAMACUE *

40. TRIPLE RATAMACUE *

A recording of the International Drum Rudiments as performed by Rob Carson, the three-time
WORLD SNARE DRUM CHAMPION, is available from Alfred Publishing Co., Inc.

STUDENT'S PRACTICE RECORD

To become a good musician you must practice every day. Find a convenient place where you can keep your instrument, book, music stand and any other practice equipment. Try to practice at the same time every day. To help you schedule your time, use this Daily Practice Record.

Name _____   Band Class (Day/Time) _____

Date	Lesson Assignment	Mon.	Tues.	Wed.	Thurs.	Fri.	Sat.	Sun.	Approved

Alfred's Drum Method, Book 1 is my go to primer for beginning percussion students. Why you ask? Because this book covers all the fundamentals I teach in one complete package. Thanks to Dave Black and the late Sandy Feldstein for setting the benchmark for introductory drum methods.

—**Steve Fidyk**
Temple University

Congratulations to Dave Black and Alfred Publishing on the 25th anniversary of a great book, *Alfred's Drum Method*, Book 1. It has to be great to have lasted 25 years with sales over 500,000 units. I know how hard it is to achieve such success. Keep rocking!

—**Carmine Appice**
Rock Legend

Every serious beginning drummer should use this book, as I consider it to be the drummer's bible.

—**Hal Blaine**
Studio Legend

Over the past 25 years, *Alfred's Drum Method*, Book 1 has become one of the most important method books to help drummers learn to play with rock-solid fundamentals. Congratulations to music biz vets Sandy Feldstein and Dave Black for collaborating on this excellent and best-selling book.

—**Steve Smith**
Drum Legend
Modern Drummer Hall of Fame

I have been using both books 1 and 2 with my students for more than 10 years. I find that *Alfred's Drum Method* clearly introduces new skills for students in a clear and logical way. Every concept is reinforced with excellent musical examples. Students find the material fun, informative, interesting, and worthy of practicing. The solos are challenging and incorporate all aspects of musical percussion, including rudiments, rolls, dynamics, repeats, and auxiliary percussion. I particularly like that I can use the Alfred method with students at every level, as there is a wealth of material suited for students of varying ability. I am so glad that *Alfred's Drum Method* is included in *Smartmusic* as well. Very often we will introduce material as a group, then allow students to practice on our workstations independently to develop their skills.

—**Chris Bernotas**
Band Director, Mountain Lakes High School, NJ

When I began teaching drum lessons 22 years ago, I was in need of an effective beginning drum book. Fortunately for me (and so many other students and teachers out there), *Alfred's Drum Method* was available. Thanks to Dave Black and Sandy Feldstein for writing a book with such a far-reaching effect. Many of my students used the book and were motivated to study further. The book is so well-structured that it showed me the way with my own future book writing.

—**Andy Ziker**
Drummer, Teacher, Author, Inventor

Alfred's Drum Method, Book 1 has served as the foundation for thousands of young drummers as they begin their musical training. Indeed, many have gone on to become respected drummers, percussionists, and successful musicians. This method has stood the test of time and is considered to be a meaningful approach for young students in their early development. It has been recommended and used successfully for decades.

—**Jim Petercsak**
SUNY Distinguished Teaching Professor
University Scholar
Lifetime Achieve Award — Past President PAS
Distinguished Alumni Award — Manhattan School of Music
The Crane School of Music
SUNY Potsdam, NY

Thanks to Alfred for having published one of the most used and best selling beginning drum books of all time! *Alfred's Drum Method*, Book 1 is a classic, and it can be used by anyone, at any age. I recommend it to beginning students at the University of North Florida, and it is constantly being recommended by my students to their private students. Congratulations and all the best for continued success!

—**Danny Gottlieb**
Grammy Award-winning drummer
Associate Professor of Jazz Studies, University of North Florida

LOGIC—"THE FORMAL PRINCIPALS OF A BRANCH OF KNOWLEDGE" describes *Alfred's Drum Method*, Book 1. This book contains all the necessary knowledge that is needed to develop into a solid snare drummer. Its time-tested track record attests to its importance. I have used it and highly recommend it.

—**John H. Beck**
Professor Emeritus of Percussion, Eastman School of Music

As a university professor, I am familiar with all of the method books available to music educators today. *Alfred's Drum Method* is always my first recommendation to students in our music education program. Its sequencing is logical and its technical demands are realistic, yet challenging. Completion of the method provides the student with a strong foundation to develop into a fine musical percussionist.

—**Dr. Frank Kumor**
Associate Professor of Music, Kutztown University

Twenty-five years ago, the authors set out to write what they hoped would be the finest beginning percussion instruction book available. More than 500,000 copies later, it's obvious they achieved their goal!

—**Joel Leach**
Emeritus Professor of Music, California State University, Northridge

I have been using *Alfred's Drum Method*, Book 1 in my Percussion Methods classes for close to 20 years now, and it's the perfect way to introduce young teachers to snare drum lesson material. It's got the right balance of good pacing, pedagogy, and fun stuff!

—**Kristen Shiner McGuire**
Coordinator of Percussion Studies, Nazareth College of Rochester

If there ever was a "classic" manual for teaching the basics of drumming, this is it. A timeless compendium that handles essential terminologies of music, reading, and rudiments in an approachable and concise way—a perfect tool for teaching!

—**Claus Hessler**
International Clinician
Author of *Open-Handed Playing*, Volumes I and II

I have used *Alfred's Drum Method*, Book 1 as a foundation for my private drum instruction for 15 years. The content is very well organized to keep students interested and moving forward, as well as learning all of the most important foundational concepts of drumming. Students really enjoy playing out of this book, and I really enjoy teaching with it.

—**Nate Brown**
Founder of OnlineDrummer.com

I have never seen another method book that covered such a broad scope of snare drum essentials in such a sensible and meticulously organized manner as *Alfred's Drum Method,* Book 1. It's a timeless classic and simply the go-to book for beginner students who need that all-important foundation to build upon.

—**Zoro**
World-renowned Player, Educator and Author of
The Big Gig: Big-Picture Thinking for Success,
The Commandments of R&B Drumming, and
The Commandments of Early Rhythm & Blues Drumming

For beginning students, there is no better book than *Alfred's Drum Method*, Book 1.

—**Clayton Cameron**
Brush Legend
Clayton Cameron & the Jass eXplosion

For over 21 years I have used *Alfred's Drum Method*, Book 1, written by Sandy Feldstein and Dave Black. It has served as a fantastic complement to our band method (*Yamaha Band Student*) for my percussion students. It is an extremely well-written, appropriately paced, sequential instruction book that guides the young percussionist through many styles of snare drum and percussion techniques and performance. It is the best introductory level percussion book I have ever seen!

—**Matt McKagan**
Band Director, Lindero Canyon Middle School

For 14 years I have started all my beginners with the *Alfred Drum Method* on their first lesson. The rhythms are presented in a well-sequenced order. The inclusion of the combination studies at the bottom of each page and the full-page solos every three lessons allows my students to fully synthesize what they have been introduced. As a result, my students understand rhythm well enough to consistently earn superior ratings on their festival solos, and many learn to sight-read well enough to get selected into the Florida All-State Band. Additionally, I found that when my students read rhythms confidently, they easily learn how to play mallets.

—**Ron Hughes**
Director, Treasure Coast Percussion Academy
Artist-in-Residence, Dreyfoos School of the Arts

For 25 years, *Alfred's Drum Method* has proven to be the most effective book available for starting beginning percussionists. As the author of several band methods, I have talked with many teachers who use my method but substitute *Alfred's Drum Method* for their percussion classes.

—**John O'Reilly**
Composer

There's a reason why *Alfred's Drum Method* is celebrating its 25th anniversary and has stood the test of time as the gold standard of methods for percussion. It is simply the best!

—**Dr. Peter Boonshaft**
Professor of Music, Hofstra University
Renowned Author

When I first started teaching 20 years ago, I scoured every publisher's booth at PASIC to find the best beginning snare drum method available. *Alfred's Drum Method*, Book 1 was clearly the most well-thought-out approach, covering all the necessary steps in an order that made perfect sense, with musical exercises that worked extremely well. When I started using it with my students, their progress confirmed I had made the right choice. After all these years (and many, many students), there still is no book that comes close. To me, it's a standard and a timeless gem in the world of drum books!

—**Joe Bergamini**
Performer (Broadway),
Author, and Editor (Hudson Music & Wizdom Media)

In my global travels to about 25 countries a year, I'm always asked for a book to start drummers into the first step to playing! *Alfred's Drum Method,* Book 1 is always the answer!

I have been using this teaching guide for years because it is the clearest method for getting to know the basics and learning them fast! Every student should have this in their library of learning and all teachers should be using this as a guaranteed result for success! Alfred Music Publishing…Congratulations on a masterpiece for drumming!

—**Dom Famularo**
World-renowned Player, Educator and Author

I've been using *Alfred's Drum Method*, Book 1 with my students for years with great success. I find it contains all the basic fundamentals that the beginning student needs. The content and layout are comprehensive and easily accessible to my students for their growth. I think it's an exceptional piece of work and to me it's the standard for all beginning drum methods. I recommend it to teachers everywhere.

—**Elliot Fine**
Percussionist, Minnesota Orchestra (retired)
Co-author of *4-Way Coordination*

Like any good teacher, a method book should have concepts that teach students by motivating and inspiring them. These concepts should also guide the student in understanding how to build a strong foundation for their musicality. Sandy Feldstein and Dave Black's collaboration, *Alfred's Drum Method*, Book 1, succeeds in this fashion and, with its excellent studies in reading, rhythm, rudiments, and repertoire, is a timeless resource that is effective not only for beginners but also professionals who want to stay sharp in their focus. Congratulations on 25 years of successful insight and encouragement for drummers everywhere!

—David Stanoch
Faculty, McNally Smith College of Music
Author, *Mastering the Tables of Time*

Alfred's Drum Method, Book 1 offers excellent sequencing and pacing for students, helping them to build a sturdy foundation.

—Dante R. Marmo
Assistant to the Director and Percussion Instructor,
University of Scranton

For the past 25 years, *Alfred's Drum Method*, Book 1 has provided beginning drum learners with well-organized study material for a person's growth and development, whether it be on an individual basis or within a class environment. Starting with page 12, the beginning learner is introduced to musical literacy, along with music reading and manipulative skills, for the playing of a snare drum in concert, and information about playing the concert bass drum and crash cymbals for playing in an ensemble environment. In addition, some of the study material and solo pieces could be played sitting at the drumset, coordinating the use of the hands and feet, in preparation for developing the independence needed to play in a jazz ensemble or small group.

Of particular pedagogical note is the development of sustaining note values on a snare drum, which has the learner FIRST working a double-bounce approach—NOT a multiple-bounce approach—to a predicated rhythm in developing short and long measure rolls.

—Jim Sewrey
Percussion Educator

Can you believe it has been 50 years since the *Haskell Harr Drum Method* was first published? A second drum method by Roy Burns, which was an updated version of the Harr series, is 25 years old. Now, Sandy Feldstein and Dave Black have co-authored a new method for teaching beginning drummers which intentionally combines the strengths of these milestone books.

Alfred's Drum Method is an outstanding revision of two of the world's most successful and widely used drum methods and it deserves consideration, particularly for its compactness and organization. I predict this book will be around for the next 50 years.

—James Warrick
Downbeat Magazine, December 1988

This year marks the 10th anniversary of the seminal method book *Alfred's Drum Method*, Book 1. With moderate initial sales in 1987, the popular method has steadily climbed the sales charts to its present sales status as the world's current best-seller, with no decrease in sight. Alfred Editor-in-Chief John O'Reilly puts it less modestly. "We've sold over 150,000 of these books, and at the rate we're going, *Alfred's Drum Method* should hit the quarter-million mark in the next three to five years. Anybody who's familiar with instructional drum books knows those numbers are pretty impressive!"

—Drum Business
September–October 1997

Alfred's Drum Method, Books 1 & 2 combine to present a thorough introduction to the art of snare drumming (and offer a wealth of exercise material to drumset players who may be weak readers or who may simply wish to improve their chops with work in the rudimental area). Teachers take note: Book 1, with its accompanying video, seems very contemporary in its approach to beginning drum instruction. This could provide a welcome alternative to having your new students ask you why they are studying out of a drumset "primer" written by a "noted drum educator" in 1936.

—Rick Van Horn
Modern Drummer Magazine, April 1989

Alfred's Drum Method, Book 1 is a strong fundamental beginning drum method. A private instructor would be invaluable to guide the student through the text, but this method could be used also as a supplement to any basic band method.

—Mark D. Ford
Percussive Notes, Spring 1988